Mathematical Team Games

Enjoyable activities to enhance the curriculum

Vivien Lucas

Tarquin

How to organise Mathematical Team Games

Photocopy a page of the chosen game for each team. Cut them out and then shuffle them a little. Teams can then deal them out in the normal way. Some teachers might prefer to photocopy them on to coloured paper and perhaps to laminate the sheets to give a more permanent and significant feel to the cards. I usually make seven or eight copies, each on a card of a different colour.

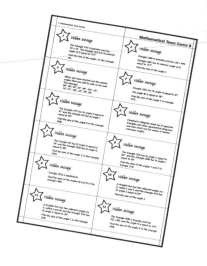

Such a method would mean that a collection of team games could be ready to use at very short notice indeed. It also means that you have a second game in reserve if the first one ends too soon.

These games have been tried on secondary school pupils from 11 to 16 with very positive feedback. In fact it was pupil enthusiasm which inspired me to put this collection together. I hope that you too will find them useful and stimulating.

Why are the Star cards numbered?

The numbers have no significance within the context of the team-game itself but are there simply to check that none of the cards are missing. In these games the final question will be found on one and possibly on two of the cards. As a positive decision in this collection, the question will never be found on card 1.

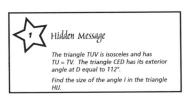

Since each card does contain some unique piece of information, a single missing card would mean that the problem cannot be solved. None of them are duds or dummies.

What is the best size for the teams?

Although in theory it does not matter if the number of cards dealt to each player is different, since the information is to be shared anyway, in practice it is better that each team member makes the same contribution. Luckily the division properties of the duodecimal system are a great help here.

Teams of three or four are probably the most satisfactory in any case and these sizes should be your first choice. If you do have to have a team of five, then it is best to insist that that the two spare cards be placed in the centre of the table.

It is of course possible to divide the class into teams of two as they would get six cards each. However, a team of two does not really encourage the social interaction that this approach to mathematical teaching is intended to produce.

Ownership of the cards

Try to encourage everyone to retain ownership of their cards and the information that they contain. The aim is to encourage cooperation and the ownership of certain pieces of information gives a status to everyone present and helps to ensure that nothing is forgotten or missed. Everyone holds some part of the jigsaw and contributes to the success of the project. In fact the process is very like tackling an ordinary jigsaw puzzle without having the picture on the box. Initially it is not immediately clear even what the problem is or how to start to work towards what the answer might be.

Sorting out the muddle and bringing order out of chaos is an important part of the satisfaction that these team-games offer.

Drawing Lots

It is probably a good idea to draw lots publicly to determine who should be in each of the teams. These team-games also act as good icebreakers for new groups or for new entrants to an established class. The randomness of the selection process helps the process of making new friends and contacts.

Competition between teams

Games like these encourage healthy competition between the teams and add an element of time pressure to finding the solution. Small edible prizes usually go down well.

How much help to give

This will depend very much on the ability of the group but I usually only allow questions along the lines of 'Is this right so far?'

Solving the problems

An important part of the value and enjoyment of these team games lies in picking out and recognising the significant pieces of information on the star-cards. Then in arranging this information and in constructing a table, chart or diagram to get to the point where the mathematics can be done and the solution found. Finally, all the information can be used and all the loose ends tied up. It will often be the case, just as in so many real life situations 'Once you can formulate the question properly, the answer is obvious'.

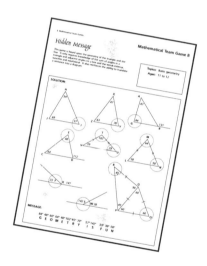

See inside the back cover for ideas about how to design mathematical team games of your own.

Magic Square

This game is based on a very special 4 x 4 magic square called a 'Diabolic' square. It uses the numbers from 1 to 16 once each and there are sums to 34 in at least 36 different ways. An active and energetic group will no doubt find other patterns which can be proposed and defended. The 36 different ways are listed below. A quick reminder about perfect squares, cubes and triangle numbers would be advisable for some classes. You might find it helpful to provide squared paper to work on.

Topics:	Primes
	Cubes
	Triangle Numbers
	Sums
Ages:	Any age

SOLUTION:

	a	b	c	d
A	1	15	14	4
B	12	6	7	9
C	8	10	11	5
D	13	3	2	16

4 Rows:

1 + 15 + 14 + 4
12 + 6 + 7 + 9
8 + 10 + 11 + 5
13 + 3 + 2 + 16

4 Columns:

1 + 12 + 8 + 13
15 + 6 + 10 + 3
14 + 7 + 11 + 2
4 + 9 + 5 + 16

4 Corner Squares:

1 + 15 + 12 + 6
14 + 4 + 7 + 9
8 + 10 + 13 + 3
11 + 5 + 2 + 16

4 Split Rows:

1 + 15 + 2 + 16
12 + 6 + 11 + 5
8 + 10 + 7 + 9
13 + 3 + 14 + 4

4 Split Columns:

1 + 12 + 5 + 16
15 + 6 + 11 + 2
14 + 7 + 10 + 3
4 + 9 + 8 + 13

2 Diagonals:

1 + 6 + 11 + 16
4 + 7 + 10 + 13

2 Split Diagonals:

15 + 12 + 5 + 2
14 + 9 + 8 + 3

1 Central Square:

6 + 7 + 10 + 11

1 Corners:

1 + 4 + 13 + 16

4 Split Row/Columns:

1 + 15 + 7 + 11
4 + 14 + 6 + 10
13 + 3 + 11 + 7
16 + 2 + 10 + 6

4 Split Column/Rows:

1 + 12 + 10 + 11
4 + 9 + 11 + 10
13 + 8 + 6 + 7
16 + 5 + 7 + 6

2 Opposite Edge Pairs:

12 + 8 + 9 + 5
15 + 14 + 3 + 2

Here are thirty-six symmetrical examples each with a total of 34.

There may be more!

Mathematical Team Game A

The even numbers are in Ac, Ad, Ba, Bb, Ca, Cb, Dc & Dd.

1 *Magic Square*

There is a two digit palindromic number in square Cc.

2 *Magic Square*

Draw a 4 by 4 square like this to fill in.

3 *Magic Square*

Your task is to complete a 4 by 4 magic square in which the numbers in each row, each column and the two diagonals all add up to 34. Each number from 1 to 16 is used just once.

4 *Magic Square*

Each square in the table is identified by a pair of letters, for example the top left square is Aa. When your square is complete, find in how many different ways you can arrive at a total of 34 using four numbers.

5 *Magic Square*

The multiples of 5 are in Ab, Cd, & Cb.

6 *Magic Square*

The prime numbers are in Bc, Cc, Cd, Da, Db & Dc
Remember that 1 is not a prime number.

7 *Magic Square*

Ac = Bc x Dc.

8 *Magic Square*

The perfect squares are in Aa, Ad, Bd & Dd.

9 *Magic Square*

Ba = Bb x Dc.

10 *Magic Square*

The perfect cubes are in Aa & Ca.

11 *Magic Square*

The triangle numbers are in Aa, Ab, Bb, Cb & Db.

12 *Magic Square*

Hidden Message

This game is based upon the geometry of the triangle and the line. It only requires knowledge of the sum of angles in a triangle and adjacent angles on a line and the words exterior, isosceles and equilateral. It also reinforces the ability to translate a sentence into a diagram.

Topics: Basic geometry

Ages: 11 to 12

SOLUTION:

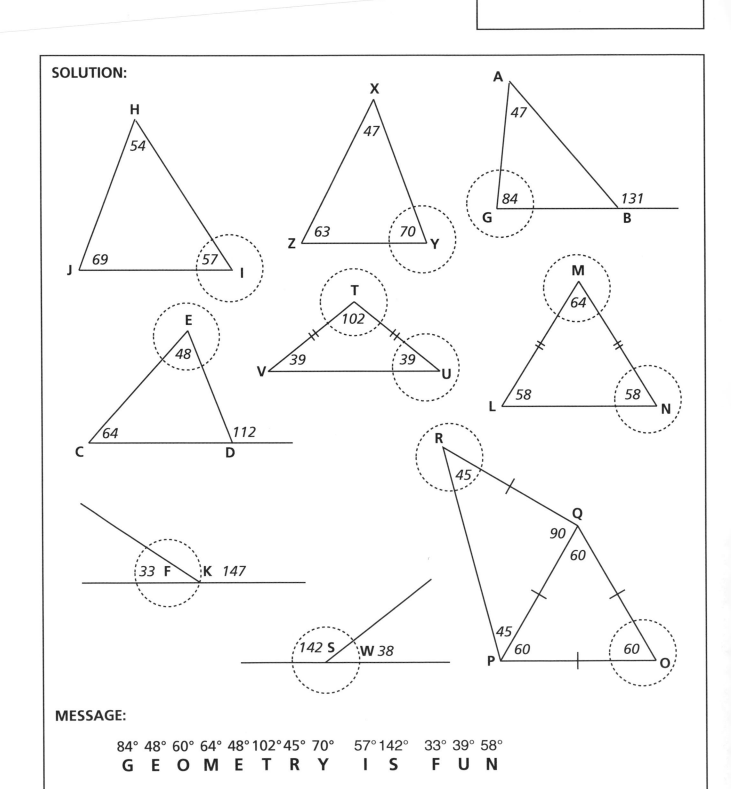

MESSAGE:

84° 48° 60° 64° 48° 102° 45° 70°   57° 142°   33° 39° 58°

G E O M E T R Y   I S   F U N

Mathematical Team Game B

Hidden Message

1

The triangle TUV is isosceles and has TU = TV. The triangle CED has its exterior angle at D equal to 112°.

Find the size of the angle I in the triangle HIJ.

Hidden Message

2

Triangle LMN is isosceles and has LM = MN.

Triangle ABG has its exterior angle at B equal to 131°.

Find the size of the angle F.

Hidden Message

3

When you have worked out the twelve angles then you will be able to de-code this message:
84°, 48°, 60°, 64°, 48°, 102°, 45°, 70°, 57°, 142°, 33°, 39°, 58°.

Hidden Message

4

Triangle ABG has its angle A equal to 47°.

The angle W is equal to 38°.

Find the size of the angle Y in triangle XYZ.

Hidden Message

5

The triangle XYZ has its angle X equal to 47° and the triangle HIJ has its angle J equal to 69°.

Find the size of the angle R in the triangle PQR.

Hidden Message

6

Construct a series of separate triangles and other geometrical diagrams and then work out the values of twelve unknown angles.

Hidden Message

7

The triangle HIJ has its angle H equal to 54° and the triangle PQR has its angle Q equal to 90°.

Find the size of the angle O in the triangle OPQ.

Hidden Message

8

The triangle CED has its angle C equal to 64° and the triangle LMN has its angle L equal to 58°.

Find the sizes of the angles T and U in triangle TUV.

Hidden Message

9

Triangle OPQ is equilateral.

Find the sizes of the angles M and N in the triangle LMN.

Hidden Message

10

A straight line has two adjacent angles on it, called F and K and the triangle XYZ has its angle Z equal to 63°.

Find the size of the angle S.

Hidden Message

11

A straight line has two adjacent angles on it, called S and W and the triangle TUV has its angle V equal to 39°.

Find the size of the angle E in the triangle CED.

Hidden Message

12

The triangle PQR is isosceles and has PQ = RQ and the angle K is equal to 147°.

Find the size of the angle G in the triangle AGB.

Garden Design

This game is a good exercise in use of mathematical vocabulary and the ability to explain clearly. All the measurements are in metres and the diagram is best constructed on squared paper where 1cm represents 0.5m. It offers practice in scale drawing, symmetry and in translating sentences into geometrical diagrams.

Topics:	Scale drawing
Ages:	11 to 12
Materials:	1cm squared paper

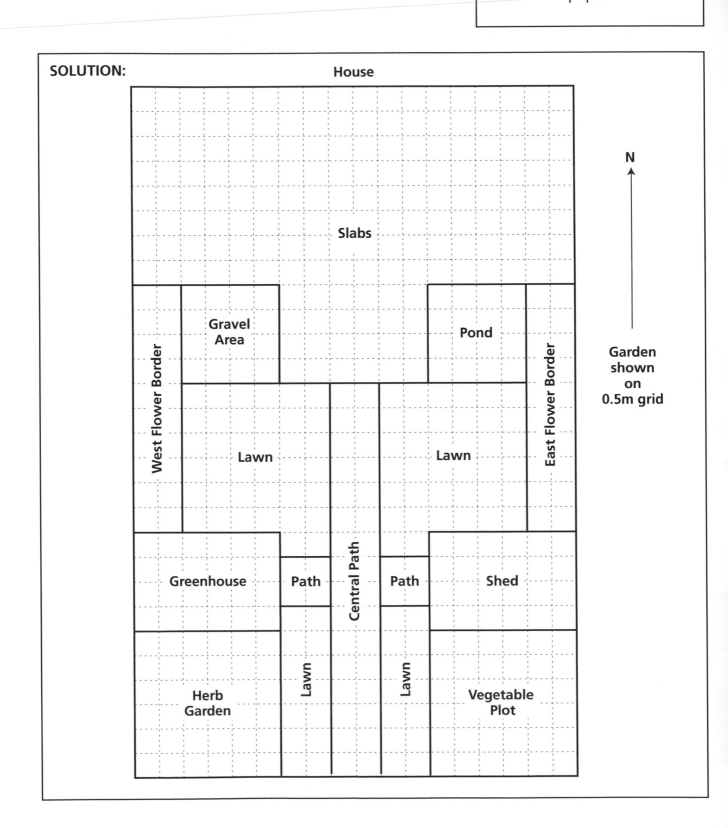

Mathematical Team Game C

There are two 1m deep flower borders next to the east and west fences which are 5m long and start from the slabbed area.

1 Garden Design

Paths lead from the central path to the doors of the greenhouse and the shed, the paths are 1m wide and the doors are situated in the centre of the 2m sides.

2 Garden Design

In the south east corner of the garden is the vegetable plot which is the same size as the herb garden and in a matching position.

3 Garden Design

The whole garden is symmetrical with the line of symmetry running down the centre of the central path. This path is 1m wide by 8m long.

4 Garden Design

There is a 2m by 2m square pond between the slabs and the eastern flower border and a 2m by 2m area of ornamental gravel between the slabs and the western flower border.

5 Garden Design

A herb garden takes up a section 3m by 3m along the south side of the greenhouse and borders the southerly fence.

6 Garden Design

Closest to the house is an area of concrete slabs laid out in the shape of a letter T. The T has a maximum height 6m and is constructed from 168 slabs, each 50cm by 50cm.

7 Garden Design

Between the herb garden and the central path is an area of lawn 1m by 3.5m and there is another matching lawn area on the other side of the path.

8 Garden Design

Your task is to work out the layout of a rectangular garden which measures 9m wide by 14m long. The house is next to the 9m side at the north end of the garden.

9 Garden Design

You need to draw a scale plan of the whole garden on 1cm squared paper. Make it 18cm by 28cm (scale 1:50) so that each concrete slab is represented by one square centimetre.

10 Garden Design

There is a greenhouse which is 3m by 2m and a shed of the same size. They are symmetrically placed equidistant from the central path.

11 Garden Design

There are matching areas of lawn either side of the central path, each with an area of 9.5m². Its shape could be divided into a 3m by 3m square and a 1m by 0.5m extra part closest to the central path.

12 Garden Design

Great Grandma's Will

This game combines dividing a number into a given ratio and dealing with fractions and percentages of sums of money. It would therefore be suitable for many lower secondary pupils. However, they might need a quick reminder if these topics have not recently been covered. The ages of the children are included in this problem in order to help with sorting the people into the right generations.

Topics:	Ratio
	Fractions
	Percentages
Ages:	11 to 13

SOLUTION:

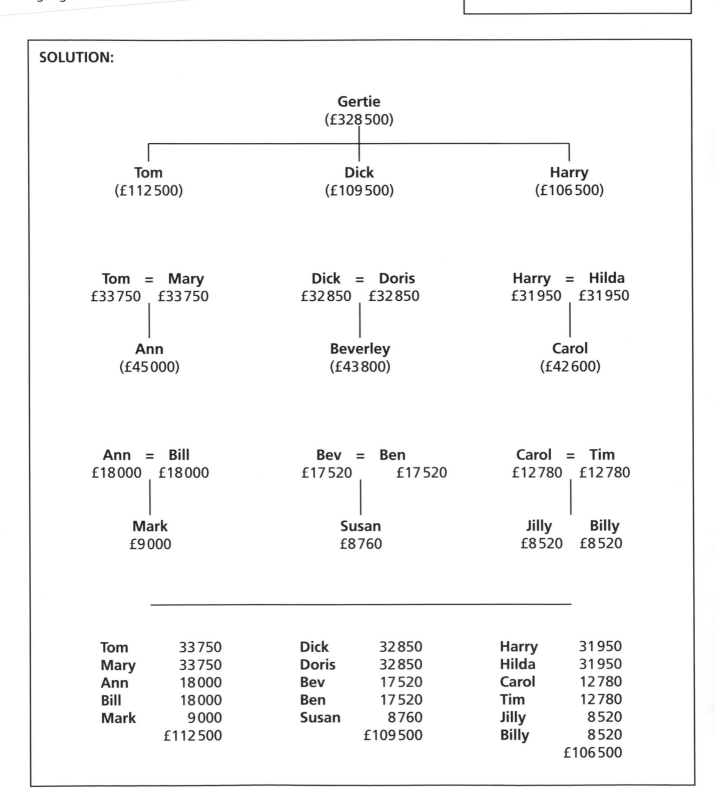

Gertie
(£328 500)

Tom
(£112 500)

Dick
(£109 500)

Harry
(£106 500)

Tom = Mary
£33 750 £33 750

Dick = Doris
£32 850 £32 850

Harry = Hilda
£31 950 £31 950

Ann
(£45 000)

Beverley
(£43 800)

Carol
(£42 600)

Ann = Bill
£18 000 £18 000

Bev = Ben
£17 520 £17 520

Carol = Tim
£12 780 £12 780

Mark
£9 000

Susan
£8 760

Jilly
£8 520

Billy
£8 520

Tom	33 750	**Dick**	32 850	**Harry**	31 950
Mary	33 750	**Doris**	32 850	**Hilda**	31 950
Ann	18 000	**Bev**	17 520	**Carol**	12 780
Bill	18 000	**Ben**	17 520	**Tim**	12 780
Mark	9 000	**Susan**	8 760	**Jilly**	8 520
	£112 500		£109 500	**Billy**	8 520
					£106 500

Mathematical Team Game D

 1 Great Grandma's Will

Great Grandma Gertie died at the grand age of 100. She had three sons and they are all still alive. Tom is 75, Dick is 73 & Harry is 71.

 2 Great Grandma's Will

Ann married Bill and they had a son Mark, now aged 15.

 3 Great Grandma's Will

Tom married Mary and they had a daughter Ann, now aged 45.

 4 Great Grandma's Will

Dick married Doris and they had a daughter Beverley, now aged 42.

 5 Great Grandma's Will

Harry married Hilda and they had a daughter Carol, now aged 36.

 6 Great Grandma's Will

After taxes had been paid Great Grandma Gertie left £328 500. She divided her money between her three sons in the ratio of their ages.

 7 Great Grandma's Will

Beverley married Ben and they had a daughter Susan, now aged 12.

 8 Great Grandma's Will

Carol married Tim and they had twins Jilly and Billy, now aged 10.

 9 Great Grandma's Will

Tom, Dick and Harry each divided up the money that they received so that each of the husbands kept 30%, each wife had 30% and each of their children had 40%.

 10 Great Grandma's Will

Draw a diagram of the family tree and work out how much they each received.

 11 Great Grandma's Will

Ann and Beverley each divided up the money that came to them so that their husbands had two-fifths, they kept two-fifths and their children had one fifth.

 12 Great Grandma's Will

Carol decided to keep 30% for herself and to divide the rest so that her husband had 30% and each of the twins had 20% of the money she received.

Coded Sentence

Fundamentally this is just a new way of testing and using the four rules of negative numbers. The questions have been printed without brackets as it seems less confusing. It might be best to point out and remind about the order of operations before starting. This is an activity best done without calculators. There are several different true statements that can be made from the ten words. Two are given below.

Topics:	Negative numbers
Ages:	11 to 13

SOLUTION:

-14	-13	-12	-11	-10	-9	-8	-7	-6	-5	-4	-3	-2	-1	0	1	2	3	4	5	6	7	8	9	10	11
A	B	C	D	E	F	G	H	I	J	K	L	M	N	O	P	Q	R	S	T	U	V	W	X	Y	Z

1a	1b	1c	1d	1e
4	-6	9	5	10
S	I	X	T	Y

2a	2b	2c	2d	2e
-2	-6	-1	6	4
M	I	N	U	S

3a	3b	3c	3d	3e
5	-6	-2	-10	4
T	I	M	E	S

4a	4b	4c	4d	4e	4F
-10	2	6	-14	-3	4
E	Q	U	A	L	S

5a	5b	5c	5d	5e
5	-7	3	-10	-10
T	H	R	E	E

6a	6b	6c	6d	6e
-2	-6	-1	6	4
M	I	N	U	S

7a	7b	7c	7d
1	-3	6	4
P	L	U	S

8a	8b	8c	8d
-9	0	6	3
F	O	U	R

9a	9b	9c	9d
-9	-6	7	-10
F	I	V	E

10a	10b	10c	10d	10e
5	-6	-2	-10	4
T	I	M	E	S

MINUS THREE TIMES MINUS FOUR TIMES PLUS FIVE EQUALS SIXTY

There are other correct possibilities

e.g. **MINUS THREE TIMES PLUS FOUR TIMES FIVE EQUALS MINUS SIXTY**

Mathematical Team Game E

1
2a: -6 + 4
4b: -10 ÷ -5
7c: 4 - -2
8d: Half of 4c
10b: -11 + 5

Coded Sentence

2
3a: -10 + 15
4a: -6 - 4
5e: -5 x 2
8b: -8 + 8
10c: Same as 2a

Coded Sentence

3
1a: 3 - -1
3b: 18 ÷ -3
5d: Same as 3d
8c: 8 + -2
10a: -10 ÷ -2

Coded Sentence

4
2b: -3 x 2
4c: -11 +17
6e: Same as 1a
7b: -1 x 3
9d: -12 + 2

Coded Sentence

5
4d: -2 x 7
5c: -9 + 12
2c: -5 ÷ 5
7d: Twice 4b
9c: -5 - -12

Coded Sentence

6
1b: -10 - -4
3c: Same as 6a
6d: -2 x -3
8a: 3 x -3
10d: Same as 4a

Coded Sentence

7
3d: -3 - 7
1e: -13 + 23
6c: Same as 2c
7a: -4 ÷ -4
9b: -9 + 3

Coded Sentence

8
9a: Same as 8a
4e: 12 ÷ -4
2d: 3 - -3
1d: -20 ÷ -4
10e: 6a squared

Coded Sentence

9
1c: -3 x -3
3e: -1 +5
5a: Half of 1e
6b: -8 - -2

Coded Sentence

10
4f: -9 + 13
2e: -2 x -2
5b: Half of 4d
6a: 8 ÷ -4

Coded Sentence

11
Write out the alphabet and then under each letter write a number starting with A = -14 up to Z = +11.

These values are needed to make ten words from the answers to the sums.

Coded Sentence

12
Each of the ten sets of coded letters, 1a,1b,1c,1d,1e etc. spells out a word.

Arrange these ten words in at least one way to make a true statement.

Coded Sentence

Games at the Fete

This game is about working out the difference between income and expenditure for two stalls at a school fete. It also introduces the ideas of probability, looking at the chances of winning a prize. Afterwards there could be some discussion about why the spinner did not produce two wins at each number.

Topics:	Profit
	Probability
Ages:	12 to 14

SOLUTION:

MARY (Spinning Wheel)

24 games each taking (6 x 30p + 6 x 50p)

The total income was £115.20

13 prizes at £1.50 = £19.50
11 prizes at £3 = £33

The total costs were £52.50

SUSAN (Tombola)

200 tickets sold at 60p each

The total income was £120

For tickets 70 and 170, 2 x £3 = **£6**

> 10, 20, 30, 40, 50, 60, 80, 90, 100, 110, 120, 130, 140, 150, 160, 180, 190, 200.

For tickets ending in zero, 18 x £2 = **£36**

> 7, 17, 27, 37, 47, 57, 67, 87, 97, 71, 72, 73, 74, 75, 76, 77, 78, 79, 107, 117, 127, 137, 147, 157, 167, 187, 197, 171, 172, 173, 174, 175, 176, 177, 178, 179.

For tickets with a 7 on, 36 x £1 = **£36**

The total costs were £78

Mary's profit was £62.70   **Susan's profit was £42**

Mary made £20.70 more profit than Susan.

COMMENTS:

In Susan's game it is unlikely that all 200 tickets will be sold because people stop buying tickets when all the prizes have been won.

The profit for the school is frequently higher than this calculation suggests because often the prizes are donated and do not have to be purchased.

Mathematical Team Game F

1 Games at the Fete

The spinning wheel has twelve sections. When the spinner stops it is equally likely to stop at any one of the numbers from 1 to 12.

2 Games at the Fete

It costs 60p to have a go on the tombola and there are 200 tickets to sell. During the afternoon, they are all sold.

3 Games at the Fete

Mary and Susan were organising stalls for their school summer fete. Mary ran the spinning wheel game and Susan did the tombola.

4 Games at the Fete

In the spinning wheel game the odd numbered prizes are worth £1.50 each and the even numbered prizes are worth £3 each.

5 Games at the Fete

If you get a tombola ticket ending with a zero you win a prize worth £2 but if you get 70 or 170 you win a £3 prize.

6 Games at the Fete

For each round of the spinning wheel game, twelve tickets numbered from 1 to 12 are sold to twelve players. The spinner is then spun rapidly and when it stops it indicates the winning number.

7 Games at the Fete

There are two prices for spinner tickets. Odd numbers cost 30p a go and even numbers cost 50p a go. In every game all twelve tickets are sold.

8 Games at the Fete

Work out how much money is taken from the players and how much is paid out in prizes for both games in order to work out which game made more profit.

9 Games at the Fete

If you get a tombola ticket which has a 7 on it you win a prize worth £1. The exceptions are 70 or 170 when you win a £3 prize.

10 Games at the Fete

Make comments on how true to life you think the two games are as they are described here.

11 Games at the Fete

During the afternoon the spinning wheel game was played twenty-four times. xThe following list shows how often each winning number came up. **1**:1, **2**:2, 3:4, **4**:2, **5**:1, **6**:3, **7**:2, **8**:0, **9**:3, 10:1, 11:2, **12**:3.

12 Games at the Fete

The tombola is like a big box filled with raffle tickets containing all the numbers from 1 to 200.

Rich, Richer, Richest

This game is essentially an exercise in solving equations where each solved equation unlocks a further one until finally the savings of all the members of the three families can be listed. Only then can the total wealth of the families be worked out and the richest discovered. Perhaps you could suggest that they use double or triple letter variables such as mrp, msp, sp, ep for the members of the Penny Family. It is valuable sometimes to realise that algebra is a tool which helps not a hurdle to climb over!

Topics:	Algebra
Ages:	12 to 14

SOLUTION:

The Spender Family are the richest.

___

The Penny Family	The Spender Family	The Banks Family
Mr Penny	**Mr Spender**	**Mr Banks**
£50 000	£70 000	£60 000
Mrs Penny	**Mrs Spender**	**Mrs Banks**
£36 000	£55 000	£56 000
Steve Penny	**Bob Spender**	**Robin Banks**
£32 000	£15 000	£16 000
Emma Penny	**Clare Spender**	**Katie Banks**
£26 000	£10 000	£13 000
£144 000	**£150 000**	**£145 000**

Mathematical Team Game G

Mrs Banks has £1000 more than Mrs Spender and £4000 less than Mr Banks.

 1 Rich, Richer, Richest

The total amount of the savings of all three families is £439000 and Clare Spender has the least at £10000.

 2 Rich, Richer, Richest

Clare Spender's savings plus Emma Penny's is equal to Mrs Penny's savings.

 3 Rich, Richer, Richest

Three families were all arguing about who was the richest. See if you can sort out the information by solving equations to find out how much each family has in the way of savings.

 4 Rich, Richer, Richest

Steve Penny's savings are twice as great as Robin Banks's and Mr Banks has four times the savings of Bob Spender.

 5 Rich, Richer, Richest

They all decided to only compare their savings as it would be difficult to work out the value of their houses and belongings. The three families were the Pennys, the Spenders and the Bankses.

 6 Rich, Richer, Richest

Mrs Spender has £5000 more than Mr Penny and £5000 less than Mr Banks.

 7 Rich, Richer, Richest

Mr Penny has £10000 less than Mr Banks and £14000 more than Mrs Penny.

 8 Rich, Richer, Richest

Bob Spender has £1000 less than Robin Banks and £2000 more than Katie Banks.

 9 Rich, Richer, Richest

Emma Penny's savings are equal to the sum of Clare Spender's and Robin Banks's.

 10 Rich, Richer, Richest

Mr Spender has saved the same amount as Bob Spender and Mrs Spender have saved together.

 11 Rich, Richer, Richest

Mrs Banks's savings plus Robin Bank's savings equals twice Mrs Penny's and Mr Banks has £60000.

 12 Rich, Richer, Richest

Three Generations

This game is a rather nice and interesting way to revise and use prime factors of quite large numbers. It is important to check that the first ten prime numbers have been listed and tabulated correctly. At least one calculator for each team will help this game forward. It has enough interest and variety without forcing so many long divisions. The anagrams will provoke some amusement but only one pair of alternatives.

Topics:	Prime factors
Ages:	Any age
Materials:	Calculators

SOLUTION:

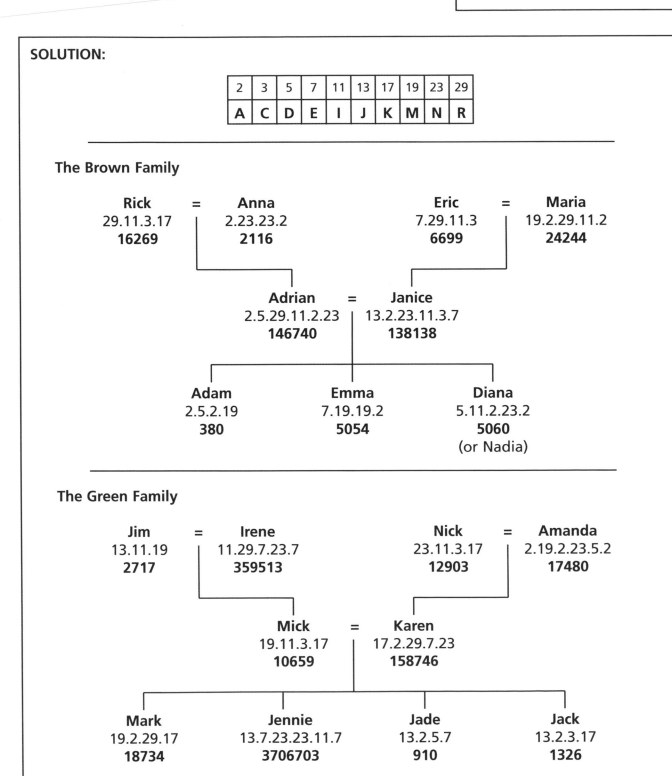

2	3	5	7	11	13	17	19	23	29
A	C	D	E	I	J	K	M	N	R

The Brown Family

Rick = Anna
29.11.3.17   2.23.23.2
16269   **2116**

Eric = Maria
7.29.11.3   19.2.29.11.2
6699   **24244**

Adrian = Janice
2.5.29.11.2.23   13.2.23.11.3.7
146740   **138138**

Adam
2.5.2.19
380

Emma
7.19.19.2
5054

Diana
5.11.2.23.2
5060
(or Nadia)

The Green Family

Jim = Irene
13.11.19   11.29.7.23.7
2717   **359513**

Nick = Amanda
23.11.3.17   2.19.2.23.5.2
12903   **17480**

Mick = Karen
19.11.3.17   17.2.29.7.23
10659   **158746**

Mark
19.2.29.17
18734

Jennie
13.7.23.23.11.7
3706703

Jade
13.2.5.7
910

Jack
13.2.3.17
1326

Mathematical Team Game H

 1 Three Generations

Match these letters in alphabetical order:
A C D E I J K M N R
with the first ten prime numbers in
ascending order to make a coding table.

 2 Three Generations

The members of the Brown and Green
families decided to apply the coding table
to each of their names and then to multiply
their prime numbers together.
For example: JEAN is 13 x 7 x 2 x 23 = 4186.

 3 Three Generations

Your task is to find the prime factors of
each person's number, to use the coding
table to change them to letters, and then
to re-arrange the letters to make a name.
Sort out the two family trees.

 4 Three Generations

In the Brown family the parents' numbers
are 146740 and 138138.

 5 Three Generations

In the Green family the parents' numbers
are 10659 and 158746.

 6 Three Generations

380 is the brother of 5054 and 5060.

 7 Three Generations

5054 is the daughter of 138138.

 8 Three Generations

The parents of 146740 are 2116 and 16269.

 9 Three Generations

There are four children in the Green family
910, 1326, 18734 and 3706703.

 10 Three Generations

17480 and 12903 are the parents of
158746.

 11 Three Generations

24244 and 6699 are the parents of 138138.

 12 Three Generations

2717 and 359513 are the parents of 10659.

Tall, Taller, Tallest

This game can be used by lower secondary pupils without any problems once the meanings of the mean, median and mode are established. These three kinds of average are only required of nine discrete items, namely the heights in centimetres of nine people. The game also uses words like perfect square, prime, palindromic, triangular etc. Pupils tend to find it useful to have a calculator available for this activity as it helps to emphasise what is meant when a number has reflective symmetry.

Topics:	Averages
Ages:	12 to 14
Materials:	Calculators

SOLUTION:

Heights

Alice	160cm	**Mean:**	169cm
Ben	163cm		
Carol	165cm	**Median:**	168cm
David	165cm		
Ellen	168cm	**Mode:**	165cm
Fiona	171cm		
Gordon	172cm	**Total of all heights:** 1521cm	
Hayley	176cm		
Ian	181cm		

Mathematical Team Game I

Hayley is 4cm taller than Gordon and 16cm taller than Alice.

1 Tall, Taller, Tallest

The median height in centimetres is the same as the number of hours in a week.

2 Tall, Taller, Tallest

Carol and David are the same height.

3 Tall, Taller, Tallest

Ben and Ian are the only two people with prime number heights in centimetres.

4 Tall, Taller, Tallest

When the people are arranged in ascending height order, they are also in alphabetical order of their names.

5 Tall, Taller, Tallest

The total of all the heights in centimetres has reflective symmetry on a calculator display.

6 Tall, Taller, Tallest

Fiona's height in centimetres is a palindromic triangular number.

7 Tall, Taller, Tallest

Your task is to work out the heights of the nine people in centimetres and then find their mean, median and mode .

8 Tall, Taller, Tallest

The mean height in centimetres is a perfect square.

9 Tall, Taller, Tallest

The range of heights is 21cm.

10 Tall, Taller, Tallest

Ian's height in centimetres is the same upside-down.

11 Tall, Taller, Tallest

Ben's height plus Hayley's height is equal to Ellen's height plus Fiona's height.

12 Tall, Taller, Tallest

Arriving at School

Before using this excellent game, it is a good idea to revise time, distance and speed problems, especially finding times in minutes for distances in kilometres at speeds in km/hr. It is also worth reminding the class of the fractions of an hour in minutes, Calculators might be allowed the first time you try this game, although the arithmetic required is not very demanding. It is much more a problem of listing and sorting and it would not be wise to choose it as the first game for a new class. It might be wise to suggest the column headings shown below.

Topics:	Distance
	Speed
	Time
Ages:	12 to 14

SOLUTION:

Name	Transport method	Distance	Speed	Time taken	Start time	Arrival time
Jenny	Walk	1 km	4 km/hr	15 mins	8.15	8.30
Una	Car	10 km	60 km/hr	10 mins	8.29	8.39
Sam	Bike	5 km	15 km/hr	20 mins	8.23	8.43
Tina	Car	10 km	50 km/hr	12 mins	8.38	8.50
Isobel	Walk	------	------	5 mins	8.29	------
------	Train	20 km	80 km/hr	15 mins	------	------
------	Walk	------	------	5 mins	------	8.54
Noreen	Walk	2 km	5 km/hr	24 mins	8.01	------
------	Bus	20 km	40 km/hr	30 mins	------	8.55
Terry	Car	15 km	60 km/hr	15 mins	8.41	8.56
Ivan	Bike	4 km	16 km/hr	15 mins	8.42	8.57
Meenal	Walk	2 km	5 km/hr	24 mins	8.34	8.58
Ella	Walk	1 km	5 km/hr	12 mins	8.38	------
------	Bus	10 km	40 km/hr	15 mins	------	9.05

The message is 'Just in time'.

Tina arrived at 8.50 and Noreen and Isobel both arrived after her so it was not possible for Noreen to talk to Isobel before Tina arrived.

Noreen and Ella did not arrive at school at the same time and were not therefore on the same bus.

Ella was the only person who was late.

Mathematical Team Game J

Arriving at School

Una and Isobel both leave home at 8.29am.

Sam and Ivan both go to school by bike

Noreen leaves home first, 41 minutes earlier than Ivan who leaves home last.

Arriving at School

Tina and Ella both leave home at 8.38am.

Jenny and Meenal both walk to school and Meenal leaves home at 8.34am.

Una goes by car at 60 km/hr.

Arriving at School

Sam cycles 5km at 1 km/hr slower than Ivan and Sam leaves home at 8.23am.

Jenny walks 1 km/hr slower than Meenal.

Una lives 10 km away from school.

Arriving at School

Noreen and Ella both go to school by bus.

Terry travels by car at the same speed as Una.

Arriving at School

On the morning in question, is it possible for Noreen to talk to Isobel before Tina arrives?

Noreen and Ella usually travel on the same bus, but do they do so this time?

Arriving at School

Meenal lives twice as far from school as Jenny and Meenal walks at 5 km/hr.

Ella lives 1 km further from school than Una.

Terry lives 15 km away from school.

Arriving at School

Ivan cycles 1km less than Sam at a speed of 16 km/hr.

The buses go at an average speed of 40 km/hr and Noreen travels twice as far as Ella does on the bus.

Arriving at School

The bus-stop is right outside the school.

Terry leaves home 1 minute before Ivan and 3 minutes after Tina.

Isobel has two 5 minute walks, one before and one after her train journey.

Arriving at School

Jenny lives 1 km from school and she leaves home 14 minutes earlier than Una.

Isobel's train journey is 20 km at 80 km/hr.

Noreen and Ella both walk at 5 km/hr from home to their bus stops.

Arriving at School

Noreen lives 2 km from her bus-stop and Ella lives 1 km from her stop.

Tina travels by car at 10 km/hr slower than Terry and lives the same distance from school as Una.

Arriving at School

School starts at 9am. Find out if anyone is late on the morning in question.

Arriving at School

Arrange the names in the order in which they arrive and the first letters of the names spell out a message.

Also work out the answers to the questions on cards 5 and 11.

Place to Place

This is a straight forward game that can be used with any pupils who have done the Theorem of Pythagoras. It only makes use of whole numbers. Some problems however do rely on using the answers from other ones and pupils may need reminding about north, south, east and west in order to get their triangles the right way round! They could either use calculators or a printed sheet of the squares of numbers up to 100.

Topics:	Pythagoras
Ages:	12 to 15
Materials:	Calculators or tables of squares

SOLUTION:

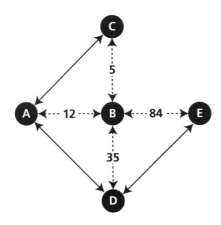

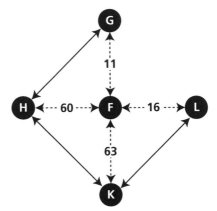

$AC^2 = 12^2 + 5^2 = 169$ **AC = 13km**

$AD^2 = 12^2 + 35^2 = 1369$ **AD = 37km**

$DE^2 = 35^2 + 84^2 = 8281$ **DE = 91km**

$GH^2 = 60^2 + 11^2 = 3721$ **GH = 61km**

$HK^2 = 60^2 + 63^2 = 7569$ **HK = 87km**

$KL^2 = 63^2 + 16^2 = 4225$ **KL = 65km**

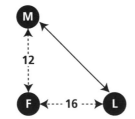

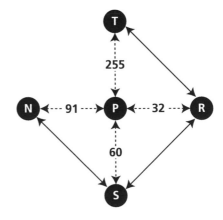

$ML^2 = 12^2 + 16^2 = 400$ **ML = 20km**

$RS^2 = 60^2 + 32^2 = 4624$ **RS = 68km**

$TR^2 = 255^2 + 32^2 = 66049$ **TR = 257km**

$NS^2 = 60^2 + 91^2 = 11881$ **NS = 109km**

$AC + AD + DE + GH + HK + KL + ML + RS + TR + NS$
13 + 37 + 91 + 61 + 87 + 65 + 20 + 68 + 257 + 109 = 808 (kilometres)

Mathematical Team Game K

Primetown is 32km due west of Radiusbury and 60km due north of Squaringham. How far is it from Squaringham to Radiusbury?

1 Place to Place

Kitefield is 63km due south of Factorham. How far is it from Kitefield to Hexadon?

2 Place to Place

When you have found ten answers, add them up to get the grand total.

3 Place to Place

Linemouth is 16km due east of Factorham. How far is it from Linemouth to Kitefield?

4 Place to Place

Addville is 12km due west of Basehampton which is 5km due south of Cubetown. How far is it from Addville to Cubetown?

5 Place to Place

Minus-on-sea is 12km due north of Factorham. How far is it from Minus-on-sea to Linemouth?

6 Place to Place

Decimalplace is 35km due south of Basehampton. How far is Decimalplace from Addville?

7 Place to Place

You will need to draw a number of separate diagrams.

All answers are in kilometres.

8 Place to Place

Evenbury is 84km due east of Basehampton. How far is Evenbury from Decimalplace?

9 Place to Place

Timeford is 255km due north of Primetown. How far is it from Timeford to Radiusbury?

10 Place to Place

Factorham is 11km due south of Gramby and 60km due east of Hexadon. How far is it from Gramby to Hexadon?

11 Place to Place

Numberton is 91km due west of Primetown. How far is it from Numberton to Squaringham?

12 Place to Place

Pages in a Book

This game is rather like an enjoyable detective investigation where the clues are expressed in the form of simple algebra. The class needs to be familiar with the expression for the nth term of a sequence. Whether the teams will actually need to formulate equations from sentences like 'Chapter Ten has one more page than Chapter Two' or will just work with the numbers is not important as the thinking is the same. However it is a good idea to encourage the use of letters and algebra where possible.

Topics:	Sequences
	Simple equations
Ages:	12 to 14

SOLUTION:

Chapter	Starting Page	End Page	No. of pages
Title	1	1	1
One	2	17	16
Two	18	31	14
Three	32	39	8
Four	40	46	7
Five	47	55	9
Six	56	64	9
Seven	65	71	7
Eight	72	88	17
Nine	89	109	21
Ten	110	124	15
Eleven	125	135	11

Total 135

Mathematical Team Game L

1 Pages in a Book

The number of chapters is a prime number. Chapter One begins on page 2 because the title page is page 1.

2 Pages in a Book

Your task is to work out exactly how many pages there are in this story book which has one title page showing the title of the book and the page numbers of the chapters. There are no blank pages.

3 Pages in a Book

The starting pages of chapters five, six and seven are the fifth, sixth and seventh terms of a sequence whose nth term is 9n +2.

4 Pages in a Book

The starting pages of chapters one, three and eight are the first, fourth and sixth terms of the sequence whose nth term rule is $2n^2$.

5 Pages in a Book

The number of pages in the last chapter is the same as the number of that chapter.

6 Pages in a Book

The even numbered chapters have a total of 62 pages.

7 Pages in a Book

Exactly three of the chapters start on page numbers that are prime numbers.

8 Pages in a Book

Exactly four of the chapters start on odd numbered pages.

9 Pages in a Book

Chapter Four has the same number of pages as Chapter Seven and one less than Chapter Three.

10 Pages in a Book

Chapter Ten has one more page than Chapter Two and one less than Chapter One.

11 Pages in a Book

The sum of the numbers of the starting pages of Chapter Ten and Chapter One is double the number of the starting page of Chapter Six.

12 Pages in a Book

Chapter One has twice as many pages as Chapter Three and one less than Chapter Eight.

Travelling Salesmen

This game is really intended for older pupils who can deal with the trigonometry of right-angled triangles. However, it could also be adapted for certain younger classes, those who would be able to solve it by scale drawing. A reminder of map scales and three figure bearings would be valuable in any case. It is so easy to get the diagrams the wrong way up. The teams should be encouraged to draw good diagrams and put all the given information on them. Calculators are needed for the trigonometry.

Topics:	Trigonometry
	Bearings
	Scale
Ages:	13 to 15
Materials:	Calculators

SOLUTION:

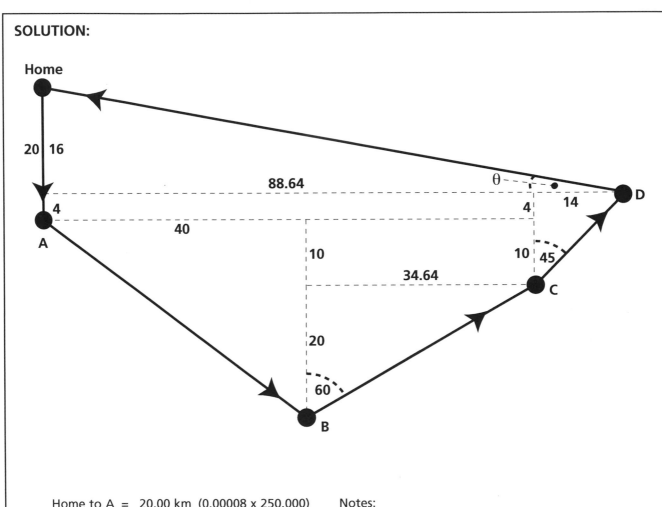

Home to A =	20.00 km	(0.00008 x 250,000)
A to B =	50.00 km	(by Pythagoras)
B to C =	40.00 km	(cos 60° = 0.5)
C to D =	19.80 km	(by Pythagoras)
D to Home =	90.07 km	(by Pythagoras)
Total =	219.87 km	
	= 220 km (3 significant figs)	

Bearing	= 280.23°	
	= 280° (3 significant figs)	

Notes:

Because B is 40.00km east of A

C is 34.64km east of B (by Pythagoras)

D is 14.00km east of C

So D is 88.64km east of A

Tan θ = 16 ÷ 88.64

So θ = **10.23°**

Dick is a travelling Dictionary Salesman who is about to retire and he is showing Harry, his replacement, his territory in Trigland.

 1 Travelling Salesmen

All towns in Trigland are joined by perfectly straight roads

 2 Travelling Salesmen

Dick always travels to the towns he visits in alphabetical order and he is encouraging Harry to do the same.

3 Travelling Salesmen

They set off from Dick's home and travel due South to Axisminster.

4 Travelling Salesmen

On the 1:250,000 map, the distance from Dick's home to Axisminster measures 8cm.

 5 Travelling Salesmen

Bodmaston lies 40km East and 30km South of Axisminster.

6 Travelling Salesmen

Chordbury is 20km further north than Bodmaston and lies on a bearing of 060° from Bodmaston.

 7 Travelling Salesmen

Dividingham lies 14km further east than Chordbury and lies in a north-easterly direction from Chordbury.

8 Travelling Salesmen

From Dividingham they return home by the shortest route.

 9 Travelling Salesmen

Draw a diagram of the journey taken and mark on it all lengths and angles known. It does not have to be to scale.

 10 Travelling Salesmen

Use trigonometry to work out the total distance travelled and the bearing required to go back to Dick's home from Dividingham.

 11 Travelling Salesmen

Do the working out to 3 decimal places and at the end give the answers to 3 significant figures.

 12 Travelling Salesmen

Old, Older, Oldest

This team game about ages requires the solution of pairs of simultaneous equations. The first task is to match up the pairs of names and to convert the sentences into equations. It might be useful to revise the formation of equations from information such as 'Susan is two years older than Mary' and 'John is twice as old as James' and so on, before embarking on this rather demanding and interesting problem.

Topics:	Simultaneous equations
Ages:	14 to 16

SOLUTION:

1.
$$A + B = 18$$
$$\underline{A - B = 8}$$
$$2A = 26$$
$$\mathbf{A = 13}$$
$$\mathbf{B = 5}$$

2.
$$2C - D = 20$$
$$\underline{C + D = 73}$$
$$3C = 93$$
$$\mathbf{C = 31}$$
$$\mathbf{D = 42}$$

3.
$$2F - E = 78$$
$$\underline{F - E = 13}$$
$$\mathbf{F = 65}$$
$$\mathbf{E = 52}$$

4.
$$3G + 2H = 38$$
$$2G + 3H = 42$$
$$9G + 6H = 114$$
$$\underline{4G + 6H = 84}$$
$$5G = 30$$
$$\mathbf{G = 6}$$
$$\mathbf{H = 10}$$

5.
$$7i - 3J = 10$$
$$3i + 4J = 147$$
$$28i - 12J = 40$$
$$\underline{9i + 12J = 441}$$
$$37i = 481$$
$$\mathbf{i = 13}$$
$$\mathbf{J = 27}$$

6.
$$5K + 2L = 43$$
$$4K + 3L = 40$$
$$15K + 6L = 129$$
$$\underline{8K + 6L = 80}$$
$$7K = 49$$
$$\mathbf{K = 7}$$
$$\mathbf{L = 4}$$

7.
$$2M + N = 91$$
$$\underline{M - N = 8}$$
$$3M = 99$$
$$\mathbf{M = 33}$$
$$\mathbf{N = 25}$$

8.
$$3\emptyset + P = 27$$
$$\underline{2\emptyset + P = 25}$$
$$\mathbf{\emptyset = 2}$$
$$\mathbf{P = 21}$$

9.
$$2R + S = 76$$
$$\underline{R + S = 47}$$
$$\mathbf{R = 29}$$
$$\mathbf{S = 18}$$

10.
$$3W - 4T = 33$$
$$2W + 3T = 107$$
$$9W - 12T = 99$$
$$\underline{8W + 12T = 428}$$
$$17W = 527$$
$$\mathbf{W = 31}$$
$$\mathbf{T = 15}$$

In order of age:

Fred	65	Satomi	18
Eric	52	Teela	15
Dawn	42	Ian	13
Mike	33	Adam	13
Wendy	31	Hayley	10
Carol	31	Kay	7
Roger	29	Gemma	6
John	27	Ben	5
Nayha	25	Laura	4
Parveen	21	Oliver	2

Mathematical Team Game N

 old, older, oldest

18 is the sum of the ages of Adam and Ben.

47 is the sum of the ages of Roger and Satomi.

 old, older, oldest

Three times Gemma's age plus twice Hayley's age is 38.

Three times Wendy's age minus four times Teela's age is 33.

 old, older, oldest

The information about the people has been mixed up, so you first have to match up the pairs of equations before you can solve them. All the answers are whole numbers.

 old, older, oldest

Three times Oliver's age plus Parveen's age is 27.

Adam's age minus Ben's age is 8.

 old, older, oldest

Your task is to discover the ages of all the people mentioned and to put them into a list starting with the oldest and finishing with the youngest. There are two sets of twins.

 old, older, oldest

Twice Wendy's age plus three times Teela's age is 107.

Three times Ian's age plus four times John's age is 147.

 old, older, oldest

Twice Carol's age minus Dawn's age is 20.

Twice Fred's age minus Eric's age is 78.

 old, older, oldest

Four times Kay's age plus three times Laura's age is 40.

Carol's age plus Dawn's age is 73.

 old, older, oldest

Twice Mike's age plus Nayha's age is 91.

Five times Kay's age plus twice Laura's age is 43.

 old, older, oldest

Fred is 13 years older than Eric.

Twice Oliver's age plus Parveen's age is 25.

 old, older, oldest

Twice Roger's age plus Satomi's age is 76.

Seven times Ian's age minus three times John's age is 10.

 old, older, oldest

Twice Gemma's age plus three times Hayley's age is 42.

Mike is 8 years older than Nayha.

Peter Power's Party

This game is intended for older pupils who are used to dealing with indices and know how to solve quadratic and simultaneous equations. Although there is not much spare time when preparing pupils for the higher level at GCSE, this particular activity is ideal if part of a group are missing and you want to gainfully employ those who remain.

Topics:	Equations
	Indices
Ages:	14 to 16

SOLUTION:

No. of people

$$27^{\frac{2}{3}} \times \frac{1}{4}^{\frac{-3}{2}} = 9 \times 8 = 7$$

Date of party

$$3c + 2d = 44 \rightarrow 9c + 6d = 132 \qquad c = 10$$
$$4c - 3d = 19 \rightarrow \underline{8c - 6d = 38} \qquad d = 7$$
$$17c = 170$$

10th July

The Angle Inn

Room $(-4)^3 + 7(-4)^2 + 3(-4) - 2$
$= -64 + 112 - 12 - 2 = £34$

Buffet $(x - 8)(x + 2) = 0 \qquad £8$ per person

Total Cost $£34 + £8 \times 72 = £610$

The Blue Cube

Room $(3w + 2)(w - 20) = 0 \qquad £20$

Buffet max of $6x - x^2 \ (x = 3)$
$y = 18 - 9 = 9 \quad £9$ per person

Total Cost $£20 + £9 \times 72 = £668$

The Compass Hotel

Room & Buffet $2q^2 - 11q - 51 = 0$
$(2q - 17)(q + 3) = 0 \qquad £8.50$ per person

Total Cost $£8.50 \times 72 = £612$

Band

$$216^{\frac{1}{3}} \times 625^{\frac{1}{2}} = 6 \times 25 = £150$$

Disco

$$16^{\frac{3}{4}} \times 25^{\frac{1}{2}} \times 27^{\frac{1}{3}} = 8 \times 5 \times 3 = £120$$

Invitations

$3y - x = 24$, when $x = 0 \quad 3y = 24 \quad y = 8p$
$8p \times 72 = £5.76$

Peter's Party was a Disco at The Angle Inn on 10th July.

Angle	Disco	Invitations	Total
£160	£120	£5.76	£735.76

Mathematical Team Game O

The cost of the buffet at The Angle Inn was £x per person where x is the positive solution to the quadratic equation
$$x^2 - 6x - 16 = 0.$$

1 Peter Power's Party

There were three possible venues: The Angle Inn, The Blue Cube and The Compass Hotel. He decided to keep the total cost as low as possible.

2 Peter Power's Party

The number of people he wanted to invite was:
$$a^{\frac{2}{3}} \times b^{\frac{3}{2}}$$
where a = 27 and b = $\frac{1}{4}$.

3 Peter Power's Party

The cost of invitations was p pence per person, where p is the intercept on the y axis of the line
$$3y - x = 24.$$

4 Peter Power's Party

He decided to hold the party on the cth day of the dth month, where c and d are the solutions of the simultaneous equations:
$$3c + 2d = 44 \quad \& \quad 4c - 3d = 19.$$

5 Peter Power's Party

Peter Power decided he wanted to have a party. He had to decide how much it would cost him, where and when to hold it and what type of music to have.

6 Peter Power's Party

The cost of hiring the room at The Angle Inn was £y where
$$y = x^3 + 7x^2 + 3x - 2$$
$$\text{and } x = -4.$$

7 Peter Power's Party

The cost of hiring the room at The Blue Cube was £w where w is the positive solution of the quadratic equation
$$3w^2 - 58w - 40 = 0.$$

8 Peter Power's Party

The cost of the buffet at The Blue Cube was £v per person where v is the maximum value of the graph
$$y = 6x - x^2.$$
(Hint: sketch it from x = 0 to x = 6.)

9 Peter Power's Party

At The Compass Hotel, the cost of the room and the buffet together was £q per person where q is the positive solution of the quadratic equation
$$2q^2 - 11q - 51 = 0.$$

10 Peter Power's Party

The cost of hiring the band with four musicians was £e where
$$e = 216^{\frac{1}{3}} \times 625^{\frac{1}{2}}.$$

11 Peter Power's Party

The cost of hiring a disco with a D.J. was £f where
$$f = 16^{\frac{3}{4}} \times 25^{\frac{1}{2}} \times 27^{\frac{1}{3}}.$$

12 Peter Power's Party

Family Tree

This is a fun game not really based on a particular topic but combining facts about how old someone was when their child was born etc. with words like perfect square, palindromic, prime, triangular etc. There may need to be some initial discussion on the meaning of these words. The information takes quite a lot of sorting out but there is sufficient to resolve the puzzle. You might offer encouragement by saying that there are just three surnames Gone, Gram and Black.

Topics:	Types of number
Ages:	Any age
Materials:	An enlargement of the blank form below

Here is Polly's unfilled in family tree, it could be enlarged to give out to pupils.

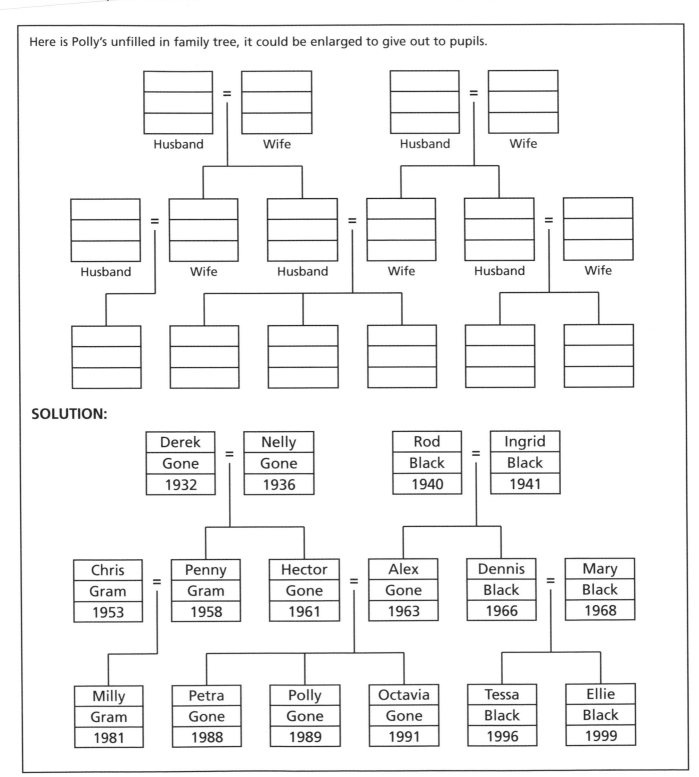

SOLUTION:

Mathematical Team Game P

1 Family Tree

Penny was born into the Gone family and married into the Gram family. She is five years younger than her husband.

2 Family Tree

Ellie is the youngest person in the family and the only person with a birth year that is a prime number. The sum of the digits is a multiple of seven. Ellie's dad is called Dennis.

3 Family Tree

The = sign is used to indicate a marriage and wives always have the same surnames as their husbands. The birth dates go in ascending order from left to right and top to bottom.

4 Family Tree

Nelly Gone was born in the only year that is a perfect square and she is 4 years younger than her husband. Ingrid Black was 58 when Ellie was born and she is one year younger than her husband.

5 Family Tree

All were born in the twentieth century and for each couple, place the husband on the left. Milly Gram is an only child. The year she was born, if turned upside down gives 41 squared in reverse.

6 Family Tree

Hector is the younger child of Derek and Nelly and his year of birth reads the same upside down. Tessa is the elder child of Dennis who was 30 when his daughter Tessa was born.

7 Family Tree

Polly Gone is the middle child of three. Her year of birth is a multiple of 9, the sum of the digits is a perfect cube and all the digits are either perfect squares or perfect cubes.

8 Family Tree

Alex is married to Hector. Her birth date includes the same digits as Nelly's but in a different order. Mary's birth year is the perimeter of a right angled triangle with its shorter sides 287 and 816.

9 Family Tree

Octavia is Polly's younger sister and she is the only person with a palindromic birth year. She is three years younger than her elder sister Petra.

10 Family Tree

Derek celebrated his 70th birthday in 2002. Dennis, who is married to Mary, was born in the year whose last two digits are the same and the sum of all four digits is 22.

11 Family Tree

Can you help Polly Gone to complete her family tree which goes back to her four grandparents. Start at the top left hand corner with the name of Polly's oldest grandfather and his year of birth.

12 Family Tree

Rod was 51 when his grand-daughter Octavia was born. Chris is married to Penny and has the only birth year that is a triangular number.

Star-card Master

☆ 1

☆ 2

☆ 3

☆ 4

☆ 5

☆ 6

☆ 7

☆ 8

☆ 9

☆ 10

☆ 11

☆ 12